Queen of Hearts

COOK BOOK

Illustrated by Josephine Irwin

THE PETER PAUPER PRESS

MOUNT VERNON · NEW YORK

Contents

HORS D'OEUVRES
to whet the Queen's appetite
page 6

ENTREES
to fill the King's stomach
page 18

VEGETABLES
for the young Knave to grow strong on
page 34

SALADS
delicate enough for a Princess
page 42

DESSERTS
your Ace in the hole
page 54

MOCK PATÉ DE FOIE GRAS

1 small can liver paté
1 can (2 ounces) chopped mushrooms
4 ounces melted butter
2 tablespoons brandy

Sauté mushrooms in a little butter until slightly brown. Do not dry out. Blend mushrooms, liver and butter, and then add brandy. Chill in refrigerator overnight. Butter will rise to the top of the crock and form a thin covering for the paté.

CLAM AND CREAM CHEESE

1 package cream cheese
½ can well-drained clams
1 teaspoon sherry
Grated onion to taste
Worcestershire sauce
Tabasco sauce

Mix well and chill. Serve on crackers. Or heat in top of double boiler and serve hot on toast.

CHEESE AND ANCHOVIES

Cut white bread into 2-inch squares, toast one side, butter the other. Put 3 or 4 anchovies on buttered side, cover with a slice of sharp cheese cut to size and broil until bubbly. Serve hot.

CHEESE ROUNDS

1 package snappy cheese
¼ cup butter
½ cup flour
Salt

Mix well and set in refrigerator until hard. Roll to thickness of pie crust, and cut into small circles with a cordial glass. Sprinkle with paprika and bake in a 350° oven 15 minutes. Serve hot. Dough may be prepared the night before for last-minute leisure.

SEAFOOD DIP

2 cups crabmeat, shrimp or lobster
1½ cups sour cream
Salt and pepper
Sweet pickle relish

Combine seafood with sour cream, add relish, season to taste. Sprinkle with chopped parsley or paprika. Serve with potato chips or crackers, as a dip.

PIGS IN BLANKETS

Use cocktail frankfurters. Make favorite biscuit recipe, rolling dough to ¼-inch thickness. Wrap each frankfurter in dough, seal with toothpick, brush with melted butter and bake in 400° oven until biscuit is brown — about 10 minutes. Serve hot.

7

SALAMI PIN WHEELS

¾ pound salami, ground
1 raw egg
2 tablespoons water
2 tablespoons prepared mustard
White bread

Put salami through grinder, and combine with remaining ingredients. Cut white bread into thin slices lengthwise, and spread with salami mixture. Roll up, and set in refrigerator, wrapped in wax paper, overnight. When ready to serve, cut into rounds, about ½ inch thick, set in pan under the broiler, and toast on one side, then on the other. Serve hot.

GARLIC AND SOUR CREAM

½ pint sour cream
1 package cream cheese
¼ teaspoon Worcestershire sauce
1 clove garlic, used to flavor bowl

Blend ingredients and serve chilled in garlic-flavored bowl with pumpernickel.

CHEESE AND BACON

Cut American cheese to fit triangles of bread which have been toasted on one side. Place cheese on untoasted side, and top with a bit of sliced bacon. Broil until bacon is crisp. Serve hot.

There's a proverb, dear Queen,
That cannot be beat;
One should eat to live,
And not live to eat!

ANCHOVY DEVILED EGGS

6 hard-boiled eggs, cut in half
2 teaspoons anchovy paste
1 teaspoon sugar
½ cup mayonnaise

Mix egg yolks with anchovy paste, sugar, and mayonnaise. Fill egg-whites with mixture. Sprinkle with very fine chopped parsley. Serve on finely shredded red cabbage, or garnished with watercress.

TARTAR SPECIAL

Mash ½ pound ground raw beef with hard-boiled egg, anchovy paste, grated onion and a little crushed garlic. Serve on rye bread or pumpernickel slices with anchovy or half olive on top.

9

BUTTERFLY SHRIMP

1 pound fresh shrimp
2 eggs
½ cup cornstarch
½ teaspoon salt

Clean shrimp. Slit halfway down back and open to look like butterfly. Beat eggs, salt and cornstarch into smooth batter. Dip shrimp carefully into batter to retain shape. Fry in deep fat (370°) until golden brown — approximately 2 minutes. Serve piping hot on colored toothpicks.

These are exceedingly decorative, but they require last-minute preparation on the part of the hostess-cook.

BRIDIE'S SPECIALTY

2 packages cream cheese
2 egg yolks
1 small grated onion
2 teaspoons baking powder
Ritz crackers

Set the cream cheese out well in advance, and when it is room temperature, blend with egg yolks and grated onion. A few minutes before serving, add the baking powder to the cream cheese mixture, blend well, and heap onto Ritz crackers. Broil for a minute or two, until bubbly and brown.

SHRIMP AND CHICKEN LIVER

½ cup shrimp
½ cup cooked chicken livers
½ green pepper
½ Bermuda onion
Mayonnaise

Force through food chopper shrimp, livers, pepper (from which seeds have been removed), and onion. Add salt and mayonnaise. Serve on toast.

NIGHT-LIFE SPECIAL

½ pint sour cream
1 small jar black caviar
Few drops lemon juice
Pumpernickel

Serve sour cream and caviar sprinkled with lemon juice in separate containers, allowing guests to help themselves to bread, cream and caviar in proportions they desire.

ANCHOVY SPREAD

6 hard-boiled eggs
3 tablespoons anchovy paste
½ cup mayonnaise

Chop hard-boiled eggs fine, blend with anchovy paste and mayonnaise and season to taste. Spread on toast.

Dear Queen, remember,
Whensoever you dine;
To eat is human,
To digest, divine!

ROQUEFORT DIP

2 packages cream cheese
Roquefort cheese to taste
1 tablespoon heavy cream
¼ teaspoon onion juice
1 tablespoon sherry

Blend all ingredients, using enough Roquefort to make a creamy consistency. Let stand a few hours before serving with potato chips or crackers. By eliminating the sweet cream, the mixture becomes a spread and may be served as such on toast or crackers.

12

HOT SARDINE CANAPÉS

1 can sardines, mashed
1 teaspoon mustard
2 tablespoons chili sauce
2 tablespoons catsup
Toast, cut into fancy shapes

Combine ingredients, and spread on toast. Broil lightly. Or place a teaspoon of the sardine mixture in a slice of bacon, roll, fasten with a toothpick and bake in 350° oven until bacon is crisp.

If a sharper mixture is desired increase the mustard to 2 teaspoons. These canapés may be prepared well in advance and broiled at the last moment.

GARDEN PLATTER WITH COTTAGE CHEESE

½ pound cottage cheese
Onion juice
Radishes
Cauliflower
White turnip
Carrots

In the center of a large round platter, heap cottage cheese seasoned with onion juice. Place radish roses, cauliflower flowerets, turnip slices and carrot strips around the cheese in decorative fashion, and allow guests to dip vegetables into cottage cheese mix.

13

SWISS CHEESE AND CLAMS

½ cup mayonnaise
½ cup milk
¾ cup grated Swiss cheese
¾ can minced clams (well drained)
Tabasco
Onion salt

Mix mayonnaise and milk. Warm slowly over a low flame and add the rest of the ingredients. Serve as dip with crackers or potato chips.

WATERCRESS CORNUCOPIAS

Remove crusts from thinly sliced white bread, butter generously with sweet butter, and roll into cornucopias, fastening with a toothpick. Place a sprig of watercress in each cornucopia so that leafy part shows. Tasty on a hot summer afternoon, accompanied by a tall glass of iced tea or coffee.

CHUTNEY AND BACON

8 strips bacon
2 tablespoons chutney

Fry bacon until crisp, chop and mix with the chutney which has been mashed with a fork. Spread on toast rounds. Makes 1 dozen. Peanut butter may be added to the mixture, if desired.

EGG-CUCUMBER-BACON

2 hard-boiled eggs
1 cucumber
1/4 pound bacon
Mayonnaise
Ritz crackers (or substitute)

Cut bacon into 2-inch pieces and fry to crispy brown. Slice hard-boiled eggs (to shape of crackers). Wash cucumber and cut slices 1/4-inch thick, same shape as eggs and crackers. Place a slice of cucumber on cracker. Place a slice of egg on cucumber and a piece of crispy bacon on top of the egg. Top with a dot of mayonnaise.

CHOPPED HERRING

1 matjes herring
1 onion
3 small apples
2 hard-boiled eggs
3 slices white bread
1 tablespoon sugar

Remove crusts of bread, soak in water and squeeze dry. Put all ingredients through grinder twice and add sugar.

Note: The herring is improved by soaking in cold water for a few hours or overnight before using to remove excess salt. Chopped herring may be sprinkled with mashed yolks of hard-boiled eggs for additional color.

HAM CORNUCOPIAS

Cut thinly-sliced boiled ham into a rectangle the size of a playing card, roll, and fasten with a strong-stemmed clove. Fill with cream cheese and pickle blended together, or whipped cream with horseradish. For the horseradish cream, use ½ cup of heavy cream, 2 tablespoons of horseradish and a dash of pepper.

HORSERADISH AND SHRIMP

½ pound cooked shrimp
1 tablespoon mayonnaise
1 teaspoon horseradish
½ teaspoon lemon juice
1 tablespoon cream
Dash of mustard

Chop shrimp which have been cleaned, cooked and shelled, and mix with other ingredients. Season to taste with salt and pepper and spread on crackers.

DEVILED HAM BISCUITS

Sift ⅔ cup flour with ½ teaspoon salt; cut in 8 tablespoons grated American cheese and 2 tablespoons butter; add 3 or 4 tablespoons milk; roll as for pastry; cut into tiny rounds; spread ham between 2 rounds; bake at 425°, for 15 minutes.

Entrees

to fill the King's stomach

ROAST TURKEY

Dress and clean turkey. Rub inside with salt and pepper. Stuff neck cavity, and then the entire breast. Fasten opening with metal pins. Fill body cavity loosely with stuffing. Rub with butter or make paste of ½ cup butter, ¾ cup flour; spread over all parts of turkey. Place turkey breast side up in open roasting pan. Drip pan from broiler may be used if large roaster is not available. Roast uncovered in slow oven (300° to 325°) 15 to 20 minutes per pound. Turkey may be placed breast side down for first half of roasting time to allow juice to run down into breast. Baste at 30-minute intervals with mixture of melted butter and hot water. When breast and legs become light brown, cover with brown paper.

BREAD STUFFING

4 cups dry bread crumbs
1 medium-sized chopped onion, if desired
1 teaspoon salt
¼ teaspoon pepper
Sage to taste
Chopped parsley
¼ teaspoon poultry seasoning, if desired
⅓ cup melted butter
Hot water or stock to moisten

Combine bread, onion, and seasoning; add

18

butter and sufficient liquid to moisten. Mix gently. Allow 1 cup stuffing for each pound of poultry or game.

ROAST GOOSE

Singe, remove pin feathers, then wash in cold water and wipe. Sprinkle with salt and pepper. Stuff with bread stuffing. Place breast side up on rack in roasting pan. Pour 2 cups boiling water over and cover. Roast 25 to 30 minutes per pound in moderately slow oven (325° to 350°), basting with fat every 15 minutes. When goose is done, garnish with cranberries and watercress, and serve with apple sauce.

ROAST CHICKEN

Dress, clean, stuff, and truss chicken. Place on its back on rack in dripping pan, rub entire surface with salt, sprinkle with pepper, and spread breast and legs with butter, rubbed until creamy and mixed with 2 tablespoons flour. Dredge bottom of pan with flour. Place in hot oven (450°) and when flour is well browned, reduce heat to moderate (350°), then baste. Continue basting every 10 minutes until chicken is cooked. For basting, use 1/4 cup butter, melted in 2/3 cup boiling water, and after this is gone, use fat in pan, and when necessary to prevent flour burning, add 1 cup boiling water.

Memo: Mix a few tablespoons of paté de foie gras or any goose liver paté into stuffing for roast hens.

BAKED CHICKEN, FLORENCE

2 broilers, cut as for frying
Seasoned flour
2 beaten eggs
Bread crumbs
½ pound butter

Dip pieces of chicken in seasoned flour, then in beaten eggs, and lastly in bread crumbs. Melt butter in baking dish, lay pieces of chicken in melted butter, and bake for 2 hours at 350°, turning chicken once so that both sides are properly browned, and increasing heat to 500° 10 minutes before serving to make chicken crisp. Serves 6.

Chicken may be cut in quarters, if preferred.

CHICKEN SAUTÉ

1 frying or roasting chicken
6 minced shallots
4 tablespoons butter
2 cups dry white wine
Salt, pepper

Have chicken cut up as for frying. Wipe dry

Your husband will praise you,

He'll whistle and sing;

At your elegant food That is fit for a King!

and sauté until golden in sizzling butter. Season. Transfer chicken to an ovenproof dish and sprinkle with minced shallots. Pour white wine into pan in which chicken was sautéd and allow to blend with butter and then pour all over chicken. Cover and cook for about 2 hours in a moderate oven. Serves 4. If shallots are not available, small onions minced with one small clove of garlic may be substituted.

Memo: This is a "specialty" dish, but extremely easy for last-minute serving.

PAPRIKA CHICKEN

1 medium-sized roasting chicken or fowl
2 onions
1 tablespoon butter
1 teaspoon salt
1 teaspoon paprika
1 cup canned tomatoes
1 tablespoon flour

Fry the onions to a golden brown. Add seasoning and tomatoes. Cut chicken into eighths and sprinkle with flour. Add to sauce, cover tightly and cook for about 2 hours.

CHICKEN DIVAN

1 5-6 pound fowl
Water
2 teaspoons salt
2½ cups medium white sauce
¼ teaspoon nutmeg
½ cup whipped cream
3 tablespoons sherry
1 teaspoon Worcestershire sauce
1 large bunch broccoli
1 cup grated Parmesan cheese

Place fowl on a rack in a kettle. Add about five cups boiling water and salt. Bring to boiling point, lower heat and simmer until tender. Cool in broth. While fowl is cooking, make white sauce and stir in nutmeg. Combine white sauce, whipped cream, sherry and Worcestershire sauce. Set aside. Cook broccoli, drain, and arrange in glass baking dish. Sprinkle lightly with some of the cheese. When chicken has cooled in broth, remove skin, slice breast and leg meat and arrange on cheese-sprinkled broccoli. Pour the sauce over all. Sprinkle generously with remaining cheese. Broil until browned and bubbly about 5 inches below high broiler flame. Serves 6.

CROWN ROAST OF PORK

Have crown of 12 chops made at market. Season with salt and pepper. Place in roasting pan bone ends up; wrap with salt pork or bacon to prevent charring; fill with favorite stuffing. Roast uncovered in 350° oven 30 minutes per pound.

To serve, remove fat from bone ends. Place paper frills over bone ends. If stuffing is not used, place roast in pan with bone ends down so fat from roast bastes rib ends. Center may be filled with browned potatoes or other vegetables at time of serving. Serves 8 to 10.

BAKED VIRGINIA HAM

Place ham fat side up on rack in open roasting pan. Do not cover. Bake in 350° oven,

The King is a gourmand,
The King is a glutton;
Just watch him devour
The whole leg of mutton!

without water, allowing 15 to 20 minutes per
pound for a large ham; 20 to 25 minutes for
a small ham; and 25 to 30 minutes for a half
ham. (The shorter times are for tenderized
hams.) Roast meat thermometer registers
170° when ham is done; 160° for tenderized
hams. Ham may be basted during cooking
period with honey, sirup from canned fruit
or cider. For the last half hour of baking, rub
surface with dry mustard and brown sugar
moistened with ham drippings. Score fat in
diamond pattern; stick a whole clove in each
diamond.

24

CANDIED HAM GARNI

Bake tenderized ham, according to preceding recipe. Remove rind (if any) and pour over sirup made of ½ cup orange juice. Return to moderately hot oven (375°) 20 minutes. Decorate with *Candied Orange Daisies:* Cut orange peel petals; cook in hot water 10 minutes. Drain; again cover with hot water; simmer until tender. Cook in sirup of 2 cups sugar and 1 cup water until translucent. Arrange petals on ham; fasten in place with cloves. Make the flower centers with green gumdrops. Serves 24.

HAM GRAVY

½ cup raisins
1 cup water
5 cloves
¾ cup brown sugar
1 teaspoon cornstarch
¼ teaspoon salt
Pinch of pepper
1 tablespoon butter
1 tablespoon vinegar
¼ teaspoon Worcestershire sauce

Cover raisins with water, add cloves and let simmer 10 minutes. Mix sugar, starch, salt, pepper, and stir into mixture until slightly thick. Then add the rest of the ingredients and simmer a few minutes before serving.

MUSTARD CREAM SAUCE

Mustard cream sauce is a good sauce for left-over or cold ham. Blend 2 tablespoons of dry mustard with water until it is of the consistency of thick cream. Into this paste fold ½ cup thick cream or evaporated milk, whipped. Season with lemon juice, salt and pepper and beat until smooth.

STANDING RIB ROAST

Select a 2- or 3-rib standing rib roast. Place the meat with fat side up in roasting pan; season with salt and pepper and place in moderate oven (350°). Do not cover and do not add water. Allow 18 to 20 minutes per pound for rare roast, 22 to 25 minutes per pound for medium, and 27 to 30 minutes per pound for well-done roasts.

ROAST LEG OF LAMB

Select a plump leg, 7-9 pounds. Wipe lamb thoroughly. Rub well with salt, pepper, flour, and very liberally with ginger. Place in uncovered pan, sprinkle with herbs (as marjoram, savory — or anything on the herb shelf). This may be varied by sprinkling with dried mint instead of herbs.

While roasting, baste with apple juice or

strong black coffee. Guaranteed to disguise the lamb and keep friends guessing.

Roast for 20 minutes at 500°, then lower to 325° for 2½ hours or more (depending on size). Or roast at 350° throughout.

BOEUF À LA MODE

4 to 5 pounds boneless pot roast
1 tablespoon salt
Pepper to taste
1 pint dry red wine
2 tablespoons fat
2 tablespoons flour
Veal knucklebone
1 quart stock or water
1 cup canned tomatoes
1 clove garlic
Dash thyme
½ bay leaf
Faggot (few sprigs parsley, stalk celery
   and leek, tied together)
5 to 6 carrots, cut in pieces
12 small onions, browned in a little butter

Lard roast with a little fat, season with salt and pepper, and let soak in wine in a refrigerator for 6 hours, turning the meat over several times. Dry meat well and brown in fat that has been heated in kettle. Drain off fat when roast is golden. Sprinkle flour in bottom of kettle and mix with the brown juice from the roast. Add bone, wine, stock, tomatoes, garlic, herbs and faggot. The meat should be just covered with liquid, no more. Bring to a boil, cover kettle, reduce heat and cook slowly on a top burner 3 to 4 hours, or until roast is almost tender. Remove meat and bone from gravy. Skim off all fat from gravy and strain. Clean pan and put back meat with carrots, onions and gravy. Simmer 20 to 30 minutes or until vegetables and meat are tender.

SHERRY HAMBURGERS

1 pound round steak, ground
⅛ pound butter
Salt, pepper
Bahamian mustard
Cooking sherry

Form patties of the hamburger, using ⅓ pound meat for each patty. Heat butter in a frying pan until it is golden brown. Fry the hamburgers until well-browned on a very hot fire, applying salt, pepper and a liberal coating of Bahamian mustard to the exposed raw side of the hamburgers. Turn over, and pour a little sherry over each hamburger. Sherry will trickle down and mix with the browned butter to make a delicious gravy. Cook about 5 minutes and serve immediately. Serves 3.

CHINESE PEPPER STEAK

1 pound flank steak
1 pound green peppers
1 pound tomatoes
½ pound onions
1 teaspoon salt
1 teaspoon sugar
1 teaspoon Gourmet powder
2 teaspoons soy sauce
2 teaspoons spiced black soybeans
  (Dow See), optional
2 cloves garlic
1 cup chicken broth
3 teaspoons cornstarch

Trim steak and wipe clean. Slice cross-grained to obtain thin slices 3 inches by 1 inch by ⅛ inch. Cut peppers into eighths. Cut tomatoes and onions into eighths. Crush garlic. Mix cornstarch with ½ cup of broth.

Sauté garlic in 3 tablespoons hot fat until slightly brown. Stir in flank steak, turning on high flame for 2 minutes. Pour steak into a warm bowl and put aside.

Sauté onions and peppers for 5 minutes, then add tomatoes, salt, sugar, Gourmet powder, soy sauce, ½ cup of broth. Cover and cook vigorously for 2 minutes. Add cornstarch mixture. Stir, cover, and simmer 2 minutes. Blend in steak. Serves 6.

29

STUFFED CABBAGE

2 pounds ground round steak
1 large fresh cabbage
1 cup cooked rice
1 large minced onion
Sage, salt, pepper
1 can tomatoes
2 small cans tomato paste
3 tablespoons vinegar
2 tablespoons brown sugar
15 bay leaves
3 ginger snaps

Boil cabbage, head down, in covering water. Cook for a few minutes until slightly tender. Separate leaves. Mix together steak, rice, chopped onion, sage, salt, pepper, and about 3 teaspoons paste. Fill each cabbage leaf with a generous helping of the meat mixture, fold like an envelope, and lay in a large roasting pan. When cabbage leaves and meat have been used up, cover mixture with tomatoes, paste, 1 paste can of water, vinegar, brown sugar, bay leaves and ginger snaps. Cook covered for 3-4 hours. Serves 8.

Note: Stuffed cabbage benefits from being made the day before. Just re-heat when ready to serve. Raisins and prunes may be added to the above recipe.

CURRIED LAMB WITH RICE

3 pounds lean lamb breast or shoulder,
   cut in cubes
3 tablespoons fat
Salt, pepper, bay leaf
8 whole black peppers
2 small sliced onions
1 teaspoon chopped parsley
1/3 cup flour
1½ teaspoons curry powder
2 tablespoons water

Brown meat in hot fat. Cover with boiling water; add onion, parsley, and seasonings. Cover and cook slowly 2 hours, or until meat is tender. Strain stock; reserve 2 cups. Mix flour and curry powder; add cold water and blend. Stir into stock; cook until thick. Add meat mixture. Serve with fluffy steamed rice.

BRUNSWICK STEW

Pot roast (5-6 pounds)
6 onions
2 green peppers
1 can whole tomatoes
1 can corn niblets or 4 cut corn (fresh)
Salt and pepper to taste

Prepare pot roast in regular manner. Add onions and green pepper. One hour before serving add the drained whole tomatoes, salt and pepper. Twenty minutes before serving add the corn.

BEEF STROGANOFF

2 pounds chuck beef, cut in small strips

4 onions   ½ pound mushrooms

1 can bouillon   ½ pint sour cream

Slice onions, and fry in a little butter with the strips of meat which have been rolled in flour, salt and pepper. Add bouillon, and simmer 2 to 3 hours. Peel mushrooms, and add 30 minutes before serving. Stir in sour cream just before removing from the heat. Serves 4 persons generously.

Three helpings of beans
Are too much for Jack;
When the belly is full,
The mind will go
Slack!

SQUASH AU GRATIN

5 small squash
4 tablespoons butter
2 eggs
Bread crumbs
¼ pound American cheese
Salt and pepper

Cut and boil squash. Drain and put through colander. Add butter and season. Add well-beaten eggs. Pour into buttered baking dish, cover with bread crumbs and grated cheese. Bake in moderate oven about 30 minutes, or until the bread crumbs are a golden brown.

CARAWAY CABBAGE

1 good-sized head of cabbage
10 onions
1 tablespoon butter
½ cup water
1 teaspoon caraway seeds
About 1 tablespoon vinegar
About 3 tablespoons sugar, to taste

Shred cabbage, eliminating heart and hard part. Brown thinly sliced onions in melted butter, and set aside. Place cabbage and caraway seeds in ½ cup water and boil for about 30 minutes. Add onions, vinegar and sugar, and cook for another 10 or 15 minutes. Serve with beef.

GLAZED ONIONS

18 small white onions
1 tablespoon butter
2 tablespoons sugar

Wash and peel onions; cover with water and cook until tender; drain. Melt butter and sugar; add onions and cook over low heat until golden brown, turning occasionally. Serves 6.

MUSHROOMS AND SOUR CREAM

1 pound mushrooms
3 tablespoons butter
1 cup sour cream
Salt and pepper to taste

Wash mushrooms. Place butter in skillet and sauté mushrooms. When tender add sour cream. Cook slowly until sauce is thickened. Season and serve.

CAULIFLOWER WITH ALMONDS

1 head cauliflower
½ cup salted almond meats
1 cup white sauce

Trim leaves from stalk, leaving 1 inch of stem. Steam, tightly covered, using enough water to cover stem but not touching head. Cook until tender, about 25 minutes. To

The Knave will grow strong,
The Knave will grow tall;
The cook has made spinach,
And he's eaten it all!

serve, cut off stalk and place cauliflower in serving dish. Stick almonds into cauliflower and pour over white sauce. Sprinkle with paprika.

GARLIC CREAMED POTATOES

Boil whatever quantity of potatoes you require in water in which a clove of garlic has been crushed. When potatoes are tender, drain, keeping the garlic water in which they were cooked, and cube. Using the garlic water for the liquid, make a cream sauce according to any standard recipe and pour over the cubed potatoes.

Note: If you prefer the flavor of onions to the flavor of garlic, substitute an onion cut in half for the clove of garlic in the water, and cream as above.

FRENCH MASHED POTATOES

6 potatoes
3/4 cup hot milk
4 tablespoons butter
1 teaspoon salt
1/2 teaspoon black pepper
1 tablespoon grated onion, if desired

Cook potatoes in boiling, salted water 30 minutes; drain and mash. Add milk, butter, seasonings; beat until fluffy. Add onion if desired. Serves 6 to 8.

POTATO PUFFS

2 cups cold mashed potatoes
2 tablespoons flour
Salt and pepper
1 egg
1 teaspoon baking powder

Blend well together in mixer. Drop a teaspoonful at a time into deep hot fat. Let fry until the puffs become brown. When well puffed, place on brown paper to drain. Serve at once.

BERTHA POTATOES

2 cups cold mashed potatoes
2 tablespoons flour
Salt and pepper
Yolks of 2 eggs

Blend ingredients well and shape into oblong patties. Place on greased baking dish. Sprinkle with vegetable or olive oil. Broil until golden brown and then sprinkle with paprika.

PERSILLADE POTATOES

12 to 18 small new potatoes
¼ cup melted butter
1 tablespoon lemon juice
⅓ cup minced parsley

Cook new potatoes in jackets; remove jackets when potatoes are done. Combine butter, lemon juice, and parsley; add potatoes; toss until coated. Serves 6.

BAKED STUFFED POTATOES

Cut large baked potatoes in half, lengthwise. Scoop out inside; mash; add hot milk, butter, and seasonings. Beat until fluffy; pile lightly into shells and return to oven to brown slightly. Grated cheese may be sprinkled on potatoes before returning to oven. Top with paprika for color.

CURRIED VEGETABLES

4 cups diced potatoes
1 package frozen cauliflower
2 packages mixed vegetables
12 white onions
1/4 pound butter
1/2 teaspoon curry powder
1/4 teaspoon salt
2 tomatoes
1 cup hot water

Parboil diced potatoes in salted water until nearly done. Put them in a heavy skillet with the two packages of frozen mixed vegetables, 1 package frozen cauliflower, 12 chopped white onions, 1/4 pound butter, 1/2 teaspoon of curry powder, a little salt, 2 tomatoes peeled and quartered and seeded, and a cup of hot water. Cover and simmer very gently, stirring occasionally, until vegetables are tender. Serves 12.

CHINESE RICE

1 cup rice
1 minced green pepper
1 minced large onion
1 lump fat

Wash and dry rice. Place in skillet with large lump of fat and fry gently, stirring from time to time. When golden brown, add onions and pepper which have been fried lightly in butter. Pour 2 cups boiling water over rice mixture and season. Cover and cook 20 minutes. Serves 4.

Memo: Never serve rice plain. Add a little chopped pimiento or scissored parsley for color.

BAKED EGGPLANT

1 eggplant
2 tablespoons butter
1 small grated onion
¼ cup bread crumbs
1 egg yolk
¼ pound grated American cheese

Parboil eggplant until tender, but not soft. Cut in half, crosswise. Scrape out the inside and mash with the butter, onion, bread crumbs, egg, cheese, and salt and pepper to taste. Refill shells, place in pan in oven. Baste with butter and brown in 350° oven for 40 minutes.

CUCUMBER SALAD

8 cucumbers
3 yolks of hard-boiled eggs
¾ cup sour cream
½ teaspoon vinegar
Salt, pepper

Peel about 8 young cucumbers, cut them down the middle lengthwise and remove the center part and seeds. Dice them and sprinkle with salt. Crumble the yolks of 3 hard-boiled eggs, mix with ¾ cup of sour cream, add salt and combine with the cucumbers adding finally ½ teaspoon of vinegar, and pepper.

WILTED LETTUCE

2 medium heads lettuce
1 teaspoon sugar
½ teaspoon salt
Dash of pepper
4 to 6 slices bacon
¼ cup vinegar
1 hard-boiled egg, chopped

Wash, drain and shred lettuce into a hot serving bowl; sprinkle with sugar, salt and pepper, mix with fork and let stand about 10 minutes to wilt slightly. Cut bacon in small pieces and fry until crisp; add vinegar, bring to a boil and pour over lettuce, mixing lightly with fork. Sprinkle with egg and serve at once. Approximate yield: 6 portions.

SALAD-IN-THE-BOWL

1 clove garlic
½ teaspoon salt
⅛ teaspoon coarse black pepper
¼ teaspoon dry mustard
¼ teaspoon sugar
¼ teaspoon paprika
⅓ cup salad oil
1 quart greens
2 tablespoons vinegar
2 tablespoons lemon juice

Rub salad bowl with cut clove of garlic; add sugar, salt, pepper, mustard, and paprika; blend. Mix in salad oil, beating with fork. Add salad greens — lettuce, endive, spinach, and watercress are a good combination. Toss until leaves are covered with dressing. Sprinkle with vinegar and lemon juice and complete the tossing. Serves 6.

ASPARAGUS SALAD

2 cups cooked asparagus (1-inch pieces)
6 sliced radishes
4 sliced scallions
4 tablespoons chopped watercress
¼ cup French dressing
Lettuce
Green pepper
Mayonnaise
18 cooked asparagus tips

Mix together cooked asparagus, radishes,

43

scallions and watercress; moisten with French dressing. Arrange nests of lettuce leaves on individual salad plates and heap with vegetable mixture. Cap the mound of salad with rings of green pepper, add a tablespoon of mayonnaise and place 3 asparagus tips upright in the center. Yield: 6 portions.

TOMATO SALAD MOLD

1 can tomato soup
1 cup boiling water
1 tablespoon vinegar
Pinch of salt
1 grated onion
1 package lemon jello
1 small grated clove of garlic
4 stalks diced celery
1 small jar stuffed green olives

Pour cup of boiling water over lemon jello and when it is dissolved add the can of tomato soup, salt and vinegar, stirring all until smooth. Then grate in the onion and garlic, holding grater over the bowl and allowing the juice to run into the mixture as well as the finely grated garlic and onion. Finally add chopped celery. Slice green stuffed olives and place them in the bottom of ring molds; fill these with mixture and chill.

Serve on lettuce leaves, garnished with watercress and sliced fresh cucumber.

44

The Princess is sweet,
Her figure is slender;
She breakfasts on salad
If the lettuce is tender!

PINEAPPLE-CARROT SALAD

2 boxes lemon jello
2 cups hot water
1 cup pineapple juice
1 cup cold water
2 carrots, grated
1 cup crushed pineapple

Prepare jello, adding pineapple juice as part of the liquid. Mix in grated carrots and pineapple and set in refrigerator to jell. Serve with mayonnaise thinned out with cream.

Lime jello may be substituted for the lemon, and is particularly refreshing on a hot summer day.

CHEF'S SALAD BOWL

1 head lettuce
2 tomatoes, cut in wedges
1 sliced cucumber
1 bunch sliced radishes
½ green pepper, cut in narrow strips
1 small Bermuda onion
2 hard-boiled eggs

Rub salad bowl with 1 cut clove of garlic. Make French dressing in salad bowl. Add lettuce broken into pieces. Arrange vegetables and sliced egg over lettuce. Season with salt and pepper.

ANCHOVY SALAD BOWL

½ head lettuce
½ bunch escarole
1 bunch watercress
¾ cup Swiss cheese, cut in strips
2 ounces anchovy fillets

Break lettuce into small pieces in salad bowl. Tear escarole and watercress into small pieces and add to lettuce. Arrange Swiss cheese and anchovies over top. Pour over ¼ cup French dressing; toss lightly. Serves 6.

AVOCADO SALAD

Cut avocado in half lengthwise, removing pit but retaining rind. Serve on lettuce with center cavity filled with grapefruit slices, orange slices, shrimp or crabmeat. Use French dressing for the fruit and Russian dressing for the seafood.

Or, peel avocado and cut into slices lengthwise. Serve with sliced grapefruit or orange, and French dressing.

FROZEN FRUIT SALAD

1 package (3 ounces) cream cheese
3 tablespoons mayonnaise
1 cup heavy cream, whipped
1 cup fruit: equal quantities of dates, cherries and pineapple, sliced and drained
1 tablespoon finely cut candied ginger
Dash of salt
Few drops almond flavoring
½ cup salted almonds
2 tablespoons butter
Lettuce
Mayonnaise

Mash cheese, add mayonnaise and mix until smooth. Add cream, fruits, ginger, salt and flavoring; turn into freezing tray of automatic refrigerator. Sprinkle with almonds which have been browned in oven with butter; freeze 2 to 3 hours, or until firm. Serve on crisp lettuce with mayonnaise or any desired dressing. Yield: 8 portions.

The Princess cooks
The best of all--
And so the Knave
Has come to call!

POTATO SALAD

3 cups diced hot potatoes
2 hard-boiled eggs, chopped
½ cup diced cucumbers
½ cup diced celery
2 tablespoons minced onion
1 teaspoon salt
Dash of pepper
2 tablespoons sugar
2 tablespoons vinegar
½ cup mayonnaise

Mix thoroughly and chill; sugar may be

48

omitted, and one or several of the following vegetables may be substituted for cucumbers or celery or both: diced radishes, chopped cabbage, minced pimientos, chopped green peppers or chopped sweet pickles. Approximate yield: 6 portions.

PARTY POTATO SALAD

6 large potatoes (2 quarts diced, hot)
½ cup mayonnaise
½ cup cooked fresh peas
½ cup diced, cooked carrots
2 pared and diced apples
2 stalks diced celery
2 finely chopped dill pickles
1 tablespoon chopped parsley
1 tablespoon chopped fresh dill
½ cup sour cream
5 tablespoons cider vinegar or lemon juice
1 tablespoon salt

Wash potatoes and place in boiling, salted water. Cook until tender. While still warm, peel and dice and blend with mayonnaise. Cover, and chill several hours. Add remaining ingredients and blend. Approximate yield: 8 to 10 portions.

Note: It takes several hours for the seasoning to penetrate the potatoes properly, and therefore salad made a day ahead of the party often tastes better than a freshly-made one.

MARINATED VEGETABLE SALAD

1 small cauliflower
½ Bermuda onion
½ cup sliced stuffed olives
1 green pepper, sliced
4 carrots, grated
1 raw beet, grated
Lemon juice
4 tomatoes
Watercress
French dressing
Salt and pepper to taste

Separate cauliflower into flowerets, and crisp with onion slices in lemon juice and ice water for two hours. Marinate cauliflower, carrots and beets in French dressing and arrange in bowl, decorated with watercress, sliced olives and tomatoes. Serve chilled.

CAVIAR SALAD DRESSING

½ cup mayonnaise
1 tablespoon horseradish
Squeeze of lemon juice
Small jar black caviar

Stir horseradish into mayonnaise. Mix well. Add lemon juice. Then fold in black caviar. Serve on hearts of lettuce. This quantity serves 4 persons.

FRENCH DRESSING

2 teaspoons sugar
½ teaspoon salt
½ teaspoon dry mustard
½ teaspoon paprika
¼ teaspoon black pepper
Dash of cayenne
2 tablespoons lemon juice
¼ cup vinegar
¾ cup salad oil

Put ingredients in jar; and shake well.

THOUSAND ISLAND DRESSING

2 tablespoons chili sauce
1 cup mayonnaise
½ teaspoon Worcestershire sauce
1 teaspoon chopped olives
1 teaspoon chopped pimientos

Mix together and shake well before serving.

CHEF'S SALAD DRESSING

4 ounces Roquefort cheese
⅛ teaspoon meat sauce
Juice of ½ lemon
2 tablespoons vinegar
½ cup olive oil
⅛ minced clove garlic
Salt and pepper

Crumble cheese with fork. Add remaining
ingredients; mix thoroughly. Makes ¾ cup.

RUSSIAN DRESSING

¼ cup sugar
2 tablespoons chili sauce
½ teaspoon salt
1 tablespoon finely chopped green pepper
Juice of 1 lemon
1 tablespoon vinegar
¼ cup catsup
1 tablespoon Worcestershire sauce
1 cup salad oil
¼ cup grated onion

Cook sugar and water until mixture spins a thread. Cool. Combine remaining ingredients; add sirup and shake thoroughly. Chill.

MUSTARD CREAM DRESSING

1 teaspoon dry mustard
½ teaspoon salt
2 teaspoons flour
3 tablespoons sugar
Cayenne pepper
2 egg yolks, beaten
⅓ cup vinegar
⅔ cup whipping cream

Combine mustard, salt, flour, sugar, cayenne pepper, and add to egg yolks. Add vinegar slowly. Cook over boiling water, stirring constantly until thick. Cool. Whip cream until stiff and fold in.

BAKED ALASKA

5 stiffly beaten egg whites
⅔ cup sugar
1 oblong sponge cake
1 brick ice cream, preferably rum flavored

Gradually add sugar to egg whites; beat until meringue forms peaks. Cut sponge cake 1 inch larger than ice cream brick. Place cake on wooden board; top with ice cream brick. Spread meringue over ice cream, sealing carefully to sides of cake. Bake in 400° oven until light brown, about 12 minutes. Serves 6. The secret of Baked Alaska is the thorough insulation provided by wooden board below and meringue on top and sides.

CARROT CAKE

1 cup carrot pulp
5 eggs, separated
1 cup sugar
1 teaspoon vanilla
1 cup chopped walnuts
1 pinch salt
½ pint whipped cream

Cook and strain carrots; squeeze dry. Mix egg yolks, sugar and salt and beat lightly. Stir in carrot pulp and fold in stiffly beaten egg whites. Add chopped nuts and vanilla. Bake in spring form for 45 minutes in a 400° oven. Cool. Top with whipped cream.

YEAST CAKE

½ pound butter
2 tablespoons sugar
Pinch of salt
3 egg yolks
1 envelope yeast, dissolved in
  ¼ cup water
¼ cup milk
2½ cups sifted flour
3 egg whites
1 cup sugar
1 cup broken walnut meats
½ cup raisins
Cinnamon

Cream the butter, add sugar and a pinch of salt. Separate eggs, and add the yolks which have been beaten until light in color. Then add yeast which has been dissolved in luke-warm water, ¼ cup milk, and the sifted flour. Roll into a ball and wrap in wax paper. Place in refrigerator overnight.

Next Day. Beat the egg whites until stiff, folding in 1 cup sugar when eggs are beaten. Remove dough from refrigerator and sep-arate into four parts, rolling each part into a rectangle about 8 x 16 inches. Spread egg whites onto the dough, and sprinkle with walnuts, raisins and cinnamon. Roll as for a jelly roll, and place the four rolls on a bak-ing sheet, cut side down. Allow to rise for 1 hour in a warm place. Bake at 325° for 25 minutes. Cool, and sprinkle with confectioners' sugar.

DE-LUXE CHEESE CAKE

¾ package zweiback
4 tablespoons melted butter
8 tablespoons sugar
1 pound cream cheese
1 teaspoon vanilla
¼ cup sifted flour
¼ teaspoon salt
4 eggs, separated
1 tablespoon lemon juice
1 cup heavy sweet or sour cream

Roll zweiback into crumbs, mix with melted butter and 1 tablespoon of sugar to make crust. Press crumb mixture on bottom of greased metal pan, 9 inches across and 2 inches deep. Or use spring form 9 inches in diameter. Cream the cheese with vanilla, 3 tablespoons sugar, flour and salt, till fluffy. Beat egg yolks, add to cheese mixture and beat thoroughly. Add lemon juice and cream and blend well. Beat egg whites almost stiff, add remaining 4 tablespoons sugar and whip until stiff. Fold into the cheese mixture. Pour into prepared pan and bake in a slow oven (325°) 1½ hours, or till set in center when tested with a silver knife. Chill before removing from pan. Yield: 12 portions.

The Queen has a birthday,
Let's bake her a cake;
How many helpings
Will Her Majesty take?

ALMOND TORTE

4 cups fine sugar
4 cups almonds, chopped
10 eggs, separated

2 Tbsp. light cream
Cocoa
¼ slice citron

Mix sugar and almonds well, add egg yolks,

light cream and the stiffly beaten egg whites.

Spread half the mixture in round cake form (buttered), sift the cocoa onto it (about 1/8 inch thick), distribute the finely cut citron evenly and then top with the remaining mixture. Bake in moderate oven until done. Serve either hot or cold with whipped cream. The cream may be flavored with almond extract or rum.

ORANGE NUT CAKE

1/2 pound butter
1 cup sugar
3 eggs, separated
3/4 cup sour cream
1 cup chopped nuts
Rind of 1 orange and 1 lemon
2 cups flour
Pinch of salt
1 teaspoon baking powder
1 teaspoon baking soda
1/2 cup sugar
Juice of 1 orange and 1 lemon

Cream sugar and butter, add egg yolks. Alternate sour cream and flour mixture (flour with powder, soda, and salt) and add rind of lemon and orange, and nuts; lastly, fold in stiffly beaten egg whites. Bake in 325° oven for 1 hour — preferably in ring form. When cake is removed from oven, leave cake in pan. Dissolve ½ cup of sugar with juice of orange and lemon and pour over hot cake. Leave in cake pan until liquid is absorbed.

LEMON ICE BOX CAKE

1 pint whipping cream
18 fresh lady fingers
1 cup sugar beaten with 4 egg yolks
Rind of 1 lemon
Juice of 2 lemons
1 envelope gelatin

Dissolve gelatin in ¼ cup cold water. When all soaked up fill cup with warm water and stir.

Add juice and lemon rind to beaten yolks, add gelatin mixture (no longer warm), fold in stiffly beaten whites, then stiffly whipped cream. Pour into spring form which has been lined with separated lady fingers, the rounded sides turned out, the round bottoms cut off straight. In lining bottom fill up all holes with pieces of lady fingers, to prevent seepage of lemon mixture.

Make crumbs from remaining lady fingers, brown lightly under flame in oven and sprinkle over top. Place in refrigerator. To serve, remove sides of pan, leaving bottom of pan under cake. Serves 12.

GRAHAM CRACKER CAKE

½ cup shortening
1 cup sugar
3 eggs, separated
1 cup milk
2 dozen graham crackers
2 teaspoons baking powder
1 cup chopped nuts
½ teaspoon salt

Cream shortening and sugar together. Beat egg yolks until light and add. Then add milk. Roll crackers fine. Combine baking powder and salt with crumbs and add to first mixture together with chopped nuts. Lastly, cut in beaten egg whites. Bake 35-40 minutes in a 375° oven in greased layer pans. Top and fill with whipped cream.

TINY CREAM PUFFS

½ cup butter
1 cup boiling water
1 cup enriched flour
¼ teaspoon salt
4 eggs

Melt butter in water. Add flour and salt all at once and stir vigorously; cook, stirring constantly, until mixture forms solid ball. Cool slightly. Add eggs one at a time, beating after each addition until mixture is smooth. Drop from teaspoon, 2 inches apart, onto

The Queen of Hearts
Some sunny day,
Will steal the tarts
And run away!

greased baking sheet. Bake in hot oven (450°)
15 minutes, then in 325° oven 25 minutes.
Remove with spatula and cool on rack. When
cool, cut side of each puff and fill with whipped cream, butter cream or ice cream. Makes
54 tiny cream puffs.

BAVARIAN RUM CREAM

5 egg yolks
5 teaspoons granulated sugar
Rum to taste
½ pint sweet cream, whipped
1 dozen lady fingers

Beat together yolks and sugar until light and creamy. Add rum to taste, and ½ pint cream, whipped stiff. Cut lady fingers in half lengthwise and line bowl. Pour in half the mixture, cover with a layer of lady fingers, and then with the remaining cream mixture. Chill in refrigerator for an hour or two before serving. Serves 6.

APRICOT CREAM PIE

12 ounces dried apricots
½ cup sugar
3 egg whites
½ pint sweet cream
½ pastry recipe

Stew the dried apricots, which have been allowed to soak a few hours, in enough water to cover, adding sugar. When tender, strain, allowing some of the sirup to moisten the strained apricots. Beat egg whites until stiff, and fold into the apricot mixture. Pour into crust which has been baked beforehand, and allow pie to set for 15 minutes in a 350° oven. Top with whipped cream.

QUICK SOUTHERN PECAN PIE

1 cup sugar
1/4 cup melted butter
1/2 cup corn sirup
3 well-beaten eggs
1 cup pecans
1 unbaked pie shell

Mix sugar, sirup and butter, add eggs and pecans. Fill unbaked pie shell with mixture and bake for 10 minutes at 400° then for 30 to 35 minutes at 350°. Serve either cold or hot. Delicious topped with whipped cream.

EGG NOG PIE

3 beaten egg yolks
1/2 cup sugar
2 cups light cream
1/8 teaspoon salt
1/8 teaspoon nutmeg
Rum to taste
3 stiffly beaten egg whites
1/2 recipe pastry

Beat egg yolks, sugar, and cream. Add salt, nutmeg, and rum. Fold in egg whites. Pour into 9-inch pastry-lined pie pan. Bake in 450° oven 10 minutes, then in 325° oven until firm, about 25 minutes. For a specially rich dessert, top with slightly sweetened whipped cream. Garnish pie with red and green candy flowers.

MOUSSE AU CHOCOLAT

½ pound sweet chocolate
6 eggs
6 tablespoons powdered sugar
Lady fingers

If possible, use chocolate that does not contain cocoa butter and break it into small pieces in a bowl. Pour boiling water over the chocolate to cover, and then cover the bowl with a large plate. After 5 minutes, carefully pour off the water and stir the chocolate with a fork, gradually adding the sugar while doing so. Beat the egg yolks slightly and stir them into the chocolate. Beat the egg whites stiff and fold them into the egg and chocolate mixture until thoroughly blended. Pour into a serving dish and refrigerate for at least 6 hours. Serve with lady fingers. Makes 6 portions.

The mousse may also be served in individual portions as follows: Use tall champagne or parfait type glasses. Pour a jigger of Crème de Cacao into each glass and then fill with mousse. Top with a candied violet or a whole marron glacé.